THE WORLD
TO COME

THE WORLD
TO COME

David
KEPLINGER

CONDUIT BOOKS
& EPHEMERA

ISBN: 978-1-7336020-5-1

Published by Conduit Books & Ephemera
788 Osceola Avenue
Saint Paul, Minnesota 55105
www.conduit.org

Book design by Scott Bruno/b graphic design

Distributed by Small Press Distribution
www.spdbooks.org

Cover image from *An Original Theory or New Hypothesis of
the Universe, Founded upon the Laws of Nature, and Solving
by Mathematical Principles the General Phaenomena of the
Visible Creation; and Particularly the Via Lactea* by Thomas
Wright, courtesy the Internet Archive; PSD detector destined
for NA61/SHINE at CERN and CBM at FAIR, Darmstadt,
Germany, courtesy CERN.

CONTENTS

I: POSSIBLE WORLDS

II: IMPOSSIBLE WORLDS

III: THE WORLD TO COME

For Parker and Sharon, who
"keep it alive...by passing it along"

and for Chuck Larson

In the silent, sometimes hardly moving times when something is coming near, I want to be with those who know secret things, or else alone.

—Rainer Maria Rilke

POSSIBLE
WORLDS

C'est tellement mystérieux, le pays des larmes.
—Antoine de Saint-Exupéry

PREMISE

That your shoes are two fish, a school that moves by the singular will. That the body is here, but elsewhere, too. That there exists a body of wind, one for you, one for the city, the country, the planet. That there's one wind moving all of this just so. Even the bride in the white wedding gown. And the groom in the charcoal suit. The beautiful car that's waiting for them. The vast night.

THE FIRST PERSON

I could hardly stand to be a body, before God scrapped me as I was and started over. This happened many times. Once I was much taller, like a walking cliff wall, but the heaviness of having fists and breasts and a penis and knees and a womb and feet, with veins like cottonwood roots, bore me down. I had to be burned up and begun again. Another time I was very small. I could fit into a tiny hole along the Euphrates. I had to stave off the wolf spider, God's beloved, who questioned me with three eyes. Alone in the world there was only the river, and no one to wash their long hair in it.

THE COLOR GREEN

Under the eaves the ceiling is black tarp, and worse, it is dripping a great deal of water in a puddle near my bed. Still it is summertime and the attic, hot, reeks of mildewed wood, and pine from Christmas greens that seep in wet boxes in the corners. When I climb up to their room, which is on top of the roof of the house, my parents lie calmly in their bed in the pouring rain as if everything is normal and nothing has happened, younger than before I was born. Under these conditions, my drenched father still springs with no effort at the sight of me, who has threatened what was aching to begin.

THE COLOR RED

July, red earth. The towns unwind on red roads, a necklace of skulls. I send this after giving up all hope. I'll never see the land the same again. Or rather, see it always, burning. With the death of separateness, compassion is possible. In the Axial Period, the remedy of fire washes the first sin, the mortal sin, away: which was to feel lonely. I'll never see the globe that held the heart of Crazy Horse, surrounding the dried heart like flame. But there is the sky, held in the window. There is the sun, in the brass knob of the door.

THE NAME OF GOD

When it falls into deep water, a newt will sink straight to the bottom, perfectly still, spread eagle, until it rises back and hits the surface breathing, swimming with its natural, easy strides. The word we have is *newt,* and this is strange, I have noticed how the water oddly suffers, it has no choice, I don't know what to call this, but feels a word has entered it.

SASSOFERRATO

In Sassoferrato it is the ultramarine that holds the idea of Mary, looking down at her hands, that captures the spirit of her prayer. It is a painting about the sea in love with the mountain crest, just as the mountain crest grasps how it will never know itself like the sea knows it. The sea at Carmel was similar, it surrounded the glass windows, and at night I heard colors like a musician does. My mother was dying. She was more pain than body then. And when the body receded, and then the pain, just after, slowly, what was left was pure crystal, blue salt: It was Sassoferrato who associated this color with the mother, the force of love that cradles and crashes over the thing, until it is the thing.

BONE

I come to realize, after I pick it up and look at it on Wet Mountain, I owe
this shard of bone my life. It is the hip of a small animal, or the ear of a
large one. It was either clicking as the femur rubbed the socket of the
pelvis, or it was hearing the click of approaching claws as it crouched
behind the mossy stone. Everything else has vanished, so I can't know
what was eaten, or what was heard, or whether death came by day or by
night. I cannot know (though I stood on the bone like the floorboard of a
house) who built this house.

STOMACH

When I first saw the *pietà*, it was a reproduction in a postcard that you sent me from Rome, the summer I refused to travel with you, and you desired to punish me for my mistake. So you offered the sculpture of a great wrinkled cape, made alive with the live mother and dead son. You knew me well. Like an egg I felt my heart slip off its tree-home and land with a thud in my gut. The perfect image escapes me. I always settle with the hollow heart, and another hollow organ, whose purpose is to catch whatever falls there from the platform.

DANSE MACABRE

Someone is holding out a globe of the world as it might look in the far
future, and everything is already all right, there are just no people on this
globe. If you look very closely at one of the small islands remaining, some
bees do their *danse macabre* around the undisturbed hive, the size of a
severed human head; but they have never seen a severed head with their
thousand eyes. They cover the hive like a beard; but they have never seen
a beard. They move in and out of the eyes, which to them are not eyes but
small compartments full of doors and hallways. The only other worlds
they know are flowers, some bent and rotting on the lime green fuse,
some still facing upward on the globe, inside the perfectly temperate,
empty, quiet, remarkably dark theater.

THE LARGE HADRON COLLIDER

While you sleep, the Large Hadron Collider in Geneva, Switzerland, is hard at work to infiltrate dreams. Though you may think you sit in a quiet room, a man this time named David, with a baby inside you but up high, in the heart, the baby moving its legs, its arms, in slow kicks and clenches, you are actually the subject of a dream. The protons bore into each other at unimaginable speeds to forge a small aperture, a peep hole, through which this world can briefly gaze into yours. There I can watch you, without your knowledge, hold the pregnancy so confidently, so adeptly, one might believe it is the natural way of things.

CLOTHESPIN

For you have placed a feather beside a light bulb and a stone. Also, a clothespin with teeth to grasp with. Being has no heft: we need to pin it down, make it stay. Like this feeling, things witness us.

THE METRIC SYSTEM

In the corner of the classroom I waited for the metric system to arrive. "Don't move a muscle now," our teacher said, the bell about to ring. We sat in our chairs, attached to our desks, feeling badly about it. "When will the metric system actually come?" I asked my neighbor, a girl with red shoes. "Don't you know? It's already here," she said, in a whisper.

TRANSLATION

Every so often there would be a show dubbed over in the voice of one actor who would have to perform all the parts: the old woman, the little boy who steals a peach, someone's infant crying. The voice was working very hard. He played each role with feeling. When the little boy who stole was caught red-handed, the old woman slipped hard on the eggs she was bringing home to her sick husband. Why did I find myself laughing at that? The infant could not catch its breath. Neither could the voice, losing command of the scene as he leapt from one point of view to the other, or did all the trembling dialogue at once.

FOX

I count my blessings like a fox does. I skulk like the stoles of my grandmother. In Harleysville on High Street, deep in my Catholic years, her stoles lay silent on the beds at parties, in the houses she said were too rich for her. I'm the slow reader who must say the words out loud. I hold every word in my mouth like an egg. I come from the guild of the thieves. I loathe and long for what won't have me. The way my grandmother threw the fox head, wide-eyed, over her shoulder, as she left in a huff.

TUSK

Each name is called up to the blackboard. Each child holds the chalk against the mouth, a miniature tusk that has just broken through. It is a little painful, learning how to think about such things. The teacher will wait as long as necessary, until even the slowest is finished, and each comes away with an identical sum.

BIRTHDAY

The farthest star we can see is five billion light years from my hometown, somewhere east of the city of Reading. After school my mother took me to Reading to buy a coat, already winter, fifty years ago. It was on my birthday. The star is called *Icarus* and can only be seen because it is magnified by bent space, as if by old glass in one of the old farmhouses. My birthday came and went with a thick fur hood and a padded coat, that's for certain, but now I remember so little of that time, except the effort and the money crumpled in her purse, the feeling she must have had of drowning.

"SURE ON THIS SHINING NIGHT"

You sang, you sang so sweetly, not alone, but to yourself, to the garden, in your place in the circle of chairs, as in a choir from Keats' year of plague the crickets joined, and no one really heard you singing. But you were singing, sweetly, and not alone, your thumb, close to your face, the small baton.

CHEKHOV

The snap of a harp string can signal the end of a society. A man begins to walk for no reason like an ape. Life becomes a succession of instructive monologues performed in dim light. Woodsmen chop away the only forest using axes from the early Holocene. Tragic, that the dreamers of the city never leave the provinces. Comic, that the provinces are just where they belong. No one plays the violin too well. The professor is frequently wrong about things. When the doctor arrives, it's always the wrong daughter who runs to fetch him to the hall.

THE SPECIAL CHILD

My father scraped a spoon against his bowl. My mother would sit so still I was afraid for us. She only spoke when buried under covers, her voice distressed by wool. When my father died, I used his boots for lampshades in the attic. When my mother died, I threw her hat down in the furnace. I know them as one body, lit up head to toe, upside down, walking on the sky.

THE MYTH OF CAUSALITY

We wanted to see where my sister had drawn "I lives here" behind the radiator at the Glenwood house, but the owners weren't home, were never home, so we imagined our father, younger than us, answering the door, taking us inside, where all of the furniture stood like it was, and when he led us down the wooden stairs we saw her there, my sister, poised with her crayon in hand, scratching her name on the wall where no one would see for fifty more years, and leaning down to it, we found we were guiding her hands, inscribing the words, writing our lives into each others' lives.

THE AGE OF THE PRINTING PRESS

It was the last night of the written word. I decided I would spend it drinking. Meanwhile I could only find a bottle of my mother's cold perfume, and a little vanilla extract from the highest cabinets. At the printer's shop, the press stood on its wooden rack, and there were fresh medieval inks in bottles that resembled tonics meant to cure the hair, the bitten nail, the pestilence-erupted skin. It was the last night of the written word. I knew the printer's ink would cure many things, but not for a long time. Meanwhile my drinking got worse, and the world, more and more, like cake and icing.

FOUR CHANDELIERS

To be alive requires conflict, and a watcher who's forgotten how the movie ends. There are Bijous on the back roads of the map, Altoona towns, Peorias, Shamokin towns. In the velvet chairs of the amygdala, you would like to fly away. You would like to lift a sword. Four chandeliers are lit by serotonin, dopamine, glutamate, and norepinephrine. This life requires patience. There is catharsis. There is a cost. God in disguise as the usher with flashlight, ousting the lovers.

II.

IMPOSSIBLE WORLDS

THE SEVEN SPHERES

We gradually passed through all the levels of bodily objects,
and even through the heaven itself.

—Augustine

1. *The Sun*

It is not to grow up, but to be *given the chance to grow old*, one of your
uncles said on his ninetieth, half his own size, a person crushed by light.
It is not to grow into or outward. It is to burn away, to condense, surrender,
thicken. Whatever burns by its own light will do the next right thing. Don't
waste your time grieving for the pliable knee, the blue stalk of the heart,
the sudden, wide-awake brain, which frets its way forward by thinking
backward. And to pass through the sun was the first gate, which burned
away the rest of everything you'd carried with you until now, belonging
not to you but to the other lives.

2. *The Moon*

I came here for a body and will not leave until I get one, I told the old clerk of the Moon. He was thin, he was as wan as Bartleby, staring at a point just past me. "I'd prefer not," he said, and shook his bald head. The offices were cold. I was shivering, less than naked without a body. As is expected in these kinds of interactions, the clerk pushed up his small glasses, and I began to beg. I had nothing to barter but my impeccable, perfect lack. "Have mercy on me," was all that came to mind. It was only then he sighed, as he slid the first fingernail, as small as a doge's gold ducat, across the surface of his desk.

3. *Mercury*

Whatever comes to life must learn to be fast. Whatever approaches death must learn to be slow. Whatever grows and goes forward is a student of the fast. Whatever stays in stillness is the student of the slow. On Mercury you have to go to school for that. There are classes hugely popular, taught by roaches, as well as courses few attend, taught by stones. When I finally jumped on that planet and held on for dear life, spinning with my legs draped off the edge, a stone advised me to fall far behind, drop out, be quiet, and try not to succeed. Always it's the stone to show you freedom, like Mercury, unalterable and dense, but faster than anything.

4. *Venus*

If I had really been to Venus and the gasses were fine, not too hot and not too cold, I suppose it would really have been love, and I'd still be there, walking among the low mountains, playing the banjo for you. You loved how I played the banjo for you, though you couldn't see me playing through all the smoke, and I couldn't see you loving it, and in reality, I'm not really sure if that was Venus after all. We have covered our faces with effervescent mud, we are walking on volcanic ash, and every time I turn to kiss you, I've suddenly pressed my lips against a mirror in my hands.

5. *Mars*

It was a world of pure ire, red ore, and despite all the hype the only intelligence on Mars were little microbes that swam like swinging maces. I had to go against my will, and I'm still angry: I resented the trip, the cost of it, the cold flight, the hard landing. I kept thinking I should leave, make my escape and go home, where I could look up at it again, with some distance now, twinkling, even spiritual. But I was told I had to stay, and I was handed a shield and a uniform, and part of me, like part of you, like anything as long as it lives, did stay.

6. *Jupiter*

Oh please can we go back to Jupiter, I begged them from the back of the car, but they'd stopped listening to me and trying to appease me, or trick me by making a game out of being silent a long time. Along that road far from home we had to move along, and I saw Jupiter getting smaller behind us until that unfathomable kingdom was nothing but a sphere the size of the moon in the rear view. My mother was twirling her hair and tuning the radio. Nothing was on. Where in the world are we going, she said to my father, the blue light of Jupiter on her disappearing face.

7. *Saturn*

Saturn is the most beautiful place, and its rings are composed of shards of what will happen. One of the shards is the book about the bear whose mother is waiting for him on the moon. One of the shards is the grip of a whole fist on my finger. One of the shards is my fist, gripping a finger. One of the shards is hair, black hair. One of the shards is a theatrical bow, with the bounce of the healthy spinal jelly. One of the shards: a painting of the Saint-Séverin cathedral. One of the shards is the ice of the morphine. One of the shards is the Keats read out loud, in front of the death mask, in Rome. One of the shards is the Keats read out loud, in front of the life mask, in Hampstead. One of the shards is a name. In fact, there are many names, which can't be spoken but only shine, for nothing but to shine, following with ease the natural law.

THE VOCATIVE CASE

In the dark of the sauna, someone was calling my name. It started with only a whisper, *Davidku,* the diminutive ending shortened in the vocative case, in a way that was familiar, in a way that asserted *you're special, you're the one.* My name was being called, beloved of me. I lay back on the moist wood, pupils dilating. The attendant shoveled stones onto the pit. The room pulsed with heat. Then a puff of smoke arose, like the entrance of the devil in a silent movie.

BEING

It was in Göttingen, the physicist Max Planck died. His head sank into the pillow, a hole fit perfectly to its size. And time stopped. A moment, we now know, has a seam on one side and a button on the other. Aliveness is important and what fills it is important, but Being is only a pillow. Everything else is what moves around the house while we are dreaming.

FIGURE

The man with his dollhouse figurines in Rome, on the busy roundabout, standing up a tiny father, mother, in a tiny family room, tiny cradle, a crowd eventually forming, traffic going around him, a woman with a camera crouching down to see. I had just come out of the Capitoline, miniaturized myself by the gigantic Marcus Aurelius reared up on his fake horse.

OTTER

In the west the otter is still at play, still saying, I am the medicine, I am the joy you forgot by the side of the stream forty years ago. I am the medicine bag, I am the joy, my body is the medicine bag, my body is the joy. The stream is still exactly the same.

SEDUCTION

Everything decays and falls away, and at exactly the same pace. It's all so, I'd say sexual, but this is less about desire than the opposite. Still, to watch it from the microscopic level, you'd think you're being tempted, flirted with—the atom unfastened from molecule, brass slowly pried through a buttonhole.

THE AGE OF THE ONION

The onion is a Book of Revelations, diced to proverb-size. This is the age that pours hot tears, that agitates the seeing eye. This is a waning age, already late. On the cutting board the onion, stripped and wet, lit up our dark kitchen in the city. This is the onion whose center is oneness, onionness, the union in my glass of gin. But not an age, not really, too brief for an age. It is a flash sautée, with the quick of the heat and the wine, the oil spitting back.

EXILE

All things are in exile from each other. The Umbrian stone, the book of feathers, you at the far end of the porch, me falling into the liminal, when you describe the saurian feet of a bird while flying, or the hole carved in the stone like a dinosaur's eye.

BETELGEUSE

When it is compared to our sun, the red giant Betelgeuse is a thousand times as large and of an impressive spectral type, but much more fragile, even ephemeral, most of its girth nothing more than cough syrup viscosity, as it expands and passes over hanging, uvulating worlds in space. "Aren't you afraid it will drown everything," a body out there is saying to itself, as they stand by a window, if you can call it a window, while swallowing hard, the muscles pulsing at the back of the throat, if you can call it a throat, in the dark of the mouth, if you can call it a mouth.

ACHIEVEMENT

A translator of the Bible has won a literary prize. The translator, who died in Constance in 1415, will not present at the ceremony. Guests include his silent God, some heads of elk looking down from the walls, and the panel of old judges. Now it is the dinner: fish is served. You can barely hear the wet, polite grinding of the jaws. Little is as it was on Lake Constance. There are some shuttered houses he might have recognized, sky like a deceptive cognate, or a few last holdouts in the patterns of the birds, the grammar of the trees, along the road where he was taken to the stake and made invisible.

PHOTON

It was only when their phosphorescence left us that we realized the photons had been here at all, trillions draped like a sweater over the Amish chair, or traveling as pilots on flecks of dust streaming from the barn window. The horses knew and threw back their wild eyes; the roosters knew and tried to communicate to them, or to us, the urgency. It was dark now and all of our eyes were closed, and the photons had left the world: like the blessed dead in William Blake they had ascended their cascading wave, but very quietly.

A MEMORABLE FANCY

As I was walking through the flames of Hell, I was glad to be in Hell. At least I was a mind on fire, albeit, separate, but alive. By the time I reached Philadelphia I must have looked very bad. At a crumbling church portico on Market Street, a man around my age asked if I knew when the shelter served dinner that evening. I hadn't come to eat, I said. I didn't know about any dinner. No matter what, I couldn't seem to shake this man. He followed me a long time and then we broke into a run, the ruins coursing by.

THE AGE OF RADIO

The radio was a good one and could pick up signals far away. I was in the cornfields of Pennsylvania where the station identifications began with "W." Later, I was getting stations west, where the call letters use a "K." I lay in my bed with the lights out, listening to the radio, imagining the Pacific Ocean. Next it seemed to pick up conversations. A couple arguing about something in Russian. I heard some mention of Vladivostok. A mouth chewing ice. The signal circumnavigated so far west, it came around to my own house again. I heard the voices of my parents in the next room. The long sighs of the sleeping dog. A stone, outside, doing nothing in a rainstorm.

ASTRONOMY

The astronomers, you say, can see so far into a distance, it's possible to witness the birth of everything. Yes, I say, but the earliest astronomy was a star chart for the dead. How many times have we had this debate? Across one microscopic swathe of night sky, you say, many eons of light are passing. A perfect darkness, I say, teeming with nebulae, slow, half frozen fish. What I would give to catch one of those fish, you say. What you need is a harpoon, I say. That's poetry, I say. That's astronomy, you say, and you always bow a little from the waist, like you have won this argument.

BASKET

Young André-Marie Ampère was there to witness the death of his father by guillotine, as the head fell from the body to which it belonged. Lifted from the basket, the father's eyes met his son's, sleepily, but blinking once or twice before awareness faded. Was he disgusted by this display? Was he moved by his father, the invisible link between father and son, as well as mind and body, momentarily, still there? I think he was moved: Ampère showed that parallel wires would attract, providing their currents matched. There is no place in the universe, as far as we know, that his math does not apply. It comforts me, so I parallel my spoon to the right of my knife, as is the rule, the knife facing toward the bowl.

PLACEBO

The last thing they gave my father for medicine was a placebo, because there was nothing more the doctors could do to keep him from rising away from the shined floor of the hospital, the roof, the bars and churches of our little town. As he floated off, calmly waving, they promised him he'd soon come back, though it required time, so he had to keep taking his medicine. We never learned what that medicine was. It came in a small orange bottle, like real medicine, with a cap you had to press down very firmly to remove.

BLINDNESS

I made a flawed parachute, and my small doll fell to its death, from windows and trees, again and again. I worried this would have to end someday. What if I lost interest in the sparking metal tank with rubber treads, or the shield I forged from tin foil and cardboard? What if I fell from a great height? What if I went blind? Just then, the lights in the house flickered. I believed some illness would turn me into gelatin. This was not far from the truth. My toys lived the rest of their lives in the garages of adulthood, in their boxes, while the door blinked up and down.

RULE

A thing as it is wants to stay as it is. That's not the physics of Sir Isaac Newton, in his long wig, fixed in black oils on the walls of the Royal Society, aging in each rendering, but it was true of him. As his body gets smaller and smaller, his attention turns to alchemy, the gambler who wages more and more to recover each loss. I like the Newton of middle age, because that's the age that I am now, because that's when he publishes *Optiks*, which looks at light as if it were a blood vessel, but lighter than anything, lighter than flies and cobwebs, a floating corpuscle, much lighter than gravity and all agents of change.

THE HEART

To live is to be cut away. It is an early alignment with belief, followed by suspicion's madness. It is happening to me now. I see this in the heart that you left in my heart. I see this in the ivy that you tended, left to me to prune, to follow the brickwork of the house. You culled, collided with it when you were alive: a nest of eggs gestating into tiny separate mouths that exited and entered in flashes.

SKELETON

When I saw the harp Sir Leonard Woolley made, who excavated Ur,
finally I understood the human skeleton. Here he stands with his pick
by the cave of the suicide Queen, Pu-Abi, the colonizer stabbing into
sacred ground. Like my parents did with my own skeleton, Woolley
misassembled two harps into one. This harp is a boat with the head of a
bull. If you play this, you have to turn it backwards, the bull's head butting
awkwardly into your chest. And with the other hand, plucking, you must
try to make something intrinsically broken come off beautiful.

THE CLASSICAL AGE

Almost as human as a lycanthrope's, the face of the Goliath beetle expresses a large range of feeling: melancholy, seething anger, and, even something you might say resembles hope. I remember that face on Lon Chaney Jr. when he's shot in the woods by his great love's father. The werewolf collapses against a tree, racked, a man who could use a strong drink. It's unclear if the silver bullet or the sudden sobriety is what kills him. I know there's only one way to kill a Goliath beetle. You have to slap them repeatedly in the face—to stun all that hope right out of them.

THE ROMANTIC AGE

The rooster, it turned out, was not its head. The head that saw the body fly away. Its thinking pouring from the body, through its broken spout. The head could discern no hope. But the body had a heart inherited from raptors. It gained a little last minute lift: and on its tippy-toes it traveled outward, scuttled up the non-existent ground. There sat the silent chicken house, the pit for the dog they named King. There was the stump, the oldest tree.

DOOR

Winter again and I am late to find my books, and slow to read them. I am a bad child who takes things for himself and doesn't like the cold. But I hear myself called, called to be one thing, called to decide what I am, to harden into marble. I am being called by you, as now again there is the door I am late to push open, and you, right behind me, dousing my head with a hood.

THE SECOND PERSON

You have the ladder in the stacks, the holy balustrade. From there, it is an easy climb into *The Meditations*. Up north in those books the Goths are assembling. In Rome, the martyrs pace the lion cage. There are still so many sins to be atoned for, left over from the elders, who were statues long before the author came along, expressing doubts, with talking points for pages, and hard to follow, winding arguments, often in the second person: You are not the only life. Yours was not the only world that had to come to an end.

THE WORLD TO COME

To learn to dance is to learn to control oneself.
—Fred Astaire

BEFORE SNOW

Low now in the troposphere, super-cooling nucleates the smallest particles of rain. What is it that is forming but has not yet fallen on our lives, to be shoveled, to be patted into blocks, like harsh words? What is this snow but old snow, returned from old storms? Love of my life, it will blow in with its ghosts out of the fallen empires, still in uniform, as now the first flakes seem to gather, along our window ledge, into the makings of an epaulette.

THREE TENEMENT ROOMS IN MORAVIA

First Flat: Irena's Voice

We have a word that's very difficult. Its parts skip backward on the tongue. A word as much to swallow as to say. And when you say it, you will be one of us. *Ch-te-ver-tek*. English: Thursday. *Čtvrtek*. But you must carve it, like tough meat, into parts. Why am I alive? During war (this is difficult to say) men from another city, it was Havířov, called on my mother every Thursday. Cakes, milk, bread, sometimes a bit of meat or butter, they paid her for their privileges. *Čtvrtek* was the hardest word, hardest day. I am alive because I ate the whole meal every Thursday.

Second Flat: Ferda's Voice

Over the town the stacks blew a cape made of ashes. Magic shows rely on simple faith. A man cannot be cut in two, sit up and try to walk away. A woman can't just disappear. A tongue cannot be shredded cloth, pulled out of the mouth. So beliefs instruct. The ride into Poland had many stops. They stopped in this town. They stopped over there and others waved from the platform. They asked for some to step forward. They took our hands sometimes and helped us on the train. They asked us little questions on our hopes and destinations. We believed in the trick and stepped into their boxes with the slots where the knives go in.

Third Flat: Pavel's Voice

The Dead of Winter, was the part I played. It was a small role and I never spoke. Sometime in March in 1945 my boots were stolen. With feet as cold as iron I stood sweeping snow from the tent in the last hours of the world. Where am I, where am I going, I thought, the snows of wartime passing over my head. If I keep moving, I'll live, so I will not bequeath my iron feet to anyone, therefore I have no children, no wife, no flesh to pour this heaviness into. I am still that shoeless man standing upright with his broom, brimmed with ire. But I am also myself, a softer person. The shoeless man and I are floating on a stage. We lower the broom on each side, and row, through snow, until now.

THE PROVERBS OF HELL

Hamlet's gravediggers were the first prose poets. They spoke in jokes, true outsiders, little squares of speech they dug. The sextons can say nothing of the world of time. But their timing was impeccable. I have carried some advice around so long, it has grown into my back like a hump.

HUNTER'S MARRIAGE VOW

I will sit with you under the trees, under the threshing, under the sky. Sky as soft as seal pelt. I will draw it down around you. Nothing dies for nothing. The pig on its spit, too far from the flame, cooking too slowly; the bright red cheek of our child, too close to the flame, growing too fast. My skeleton will glow against your skeleton until we both burn through, and we'll begin to see the person underneath our bodies. Who goes there? I'll ask you in thousands of ways, whenever you enter the room.

POLITENESS

I said very little during the meal. She and her father sat watching me. I remember the hard work of politeness, how it is done out of, not love, but surrender. How I sawed and sawed at the meat. How the deer did not flinch on the plate.

NAMES AND CALLINGS

You came when you heard the crunch of stones. I heard you crunching, you said. So I stopped and turned and when we paused there, a silence crossed between us like a bee shaking pollen from the anthers.

THE AGE OF TELEVISION

The dial on our Zenith television was stripped and frustrated all repairs, but this allowed me, I discovered, to view multiple channels at once: I could maneuver it a certain way, so that, in double exposure, while I was tuned in to a replay of the moon landing three weeks before, a journalist was interviewing Charles Manson in his cell, pressing the microphone into his moon face, just as the Eagle touched down on the chalky, lifeless surface of another world, a world to come, with everybody watching and listening.

NOSTALGIA

The old city with its great facades is now unbombed, the streets unrubbled. And the passengers on the Chopin Express are getting used to their small compartments. They lie down, side by side, in cramped quarters. They are not the actual passengers, who have died or were killed, but this ride is a form of nostalgia, a return to what had been a man lifting the coffee halfway to the lips—as the trees like long, clean notes play exactly to the original, highly authentic, ticking of tracks. So young are the trees, so spare. So spaced apart—as in the great rests of silence that blast open between them.

MEMORY

As neither loneliness nor togetherness, I remember my mother and father. It was more like the way these hummingbirds keep arguing or lovemaking. I can never tell. The invisible wings: flung forward by desire. The cupped tail, empty. What I remember is desire.

CENTURY

On one recording from a century ago, in the first suite, the dead cellist's bow sits perched against a hoisted bridge. He breathes deeply like my father cutting meat at our table. The sirens on this street seem to call up my childhood, too: its fantasies of jail, now on a dance of *prelude, allemande, sarabande* and *gigue*. The dead hand plays, but not only to me. It plays to my father, struggling to bore through the meat. It plays to my little boy room, to my little boy bed, my little boy belly, my breathing wooden walls and floor.

DURING SNOW

In an elevator during a snowstorm, a small crowd is thinking about snow. They don't see the snow, there are no windows, it's a very small elevator in Paris, typical gate guarding their hands from the floors they watch rising past them. They are descending like snow, toward snow. They don't hear any snow, the negative sound of the snow, how it pulls down with it some redundant hum there is no name for. But they are thinking of it, they believe it will bury them....*Je déteste la neige*, a woman who survived the war, thistle-like and crooked, announces to no one, between the third and second floor. Even as a few of them laugh, as they fall faster than the snow can fall, the woman keeps her neck stiff and straight, her eyes ahead, dead serious.

ANGELS AND WOUNDS

A play called *Angels and Wounds*, by David Keplinger, that goes on for years and has no curtain, where the author plays one of the parts. In some scenes it is the wound in him that sees the same wound in the other. What is re-enacted is an old disaster. In some scenes it is his Angel that addresses the other's wound, or it is reversed, and he is the wounded one, drawn to the Angel. Codependence casts its green light on the stage. There is hardly any dialogue except the sound of silverware, bottlecaps, slamming doors. But in some scenes, the Angel in him engages the Angel in the other. It's the same play his parents put on, and he plagiarized everything.

GAZEBO

On the subject of tenderness, let us sit and discuss for an hour under the imaginary gazebo of meaning. It is like a moment in Pietro Lorenzetti, where what Jesus teaches at the table, the little cat and dog, lapping up the extra bread, already know how to do.

DARK MATTER

Nine parts out of ten of these sentences are made of dark matter. Two sentences whose dark matter cleaves them are: I must find what I know how to do. I must do what I know how to do. I might decide to study fullness, but I need not. I might decide to study emptiness, but I need not. Vera Rubin, mother of dark matter, said, "We're out of kindergarten, but only in about third grade." What holds words on this page? It's another sentence's beginning, somewhere else, that is forming this sentence's end. I remember how it was for us, learning to loop the cursive on a piece of lined paper, tissue thin like crêpe, rehearsing the shape of my name.

ALMANAC

The dogwood in our front yard, always on the week the driving rain arrived, blossomed purple flowers fully formed. That night the petals fell, wet and pulverized. The fair had come to town. We left the house without our coats, got drenched at the top of the Ferris wheel. It was predicted in the almanac: my sister would drive a boy to tears. He couldn't get over it, crying out her name as he drove his car across our lawn. My father cut the whole tree down. And the flowers dissolved, for the last time, in chunks of flung mud.

VOYAGE

At the wrestling match when we cross the equator, the two opponents are, as always, both winning. "Then I will pour out my thoughts to you, I will make known to you my teachings," I read out loud from the Navy issue Bible I am carrying, speaking quickly like a sports announcer.

THE AMERICAN BALLET THEATER

We were dancing in the American Ballet Theater. I wore crinoline and you wore a tuxedo. Martha Graham was in the audience and we were performing spectacularly. Franklin Roosevelt stood up to let someone pass down his row. It was the King of Siam. Tyrone Power went to the bar and cocked his hat at his reflection. Fay Wray and Man Ray exchanged his Stetson for her panty hose. "Wrong Way" Corrigan described his descent into Ireland, how the biplane shuddered in the wind, how he believed the green below was California. And you were holding me, me secretly in love with you, in our pas de deux, with nobody paying attention.

THE IRON AGE

Often three at a time the hatpins held the pillbox hat to the hair, attached at the brim by an Iron Age design. The head is a teardrop of pearl, and the woman, with a face that recalled the paintings of Sargent, would sit at those circular tables in another century, along with her three small daughters, who would sometimes receive on the lower part of the thigh, just below the hem of the skirt, the quick jab, its drop of blood as perfect and round as a burial mound.

ZENO'S PARADOXES

The paradoxes of Zeno had to make their way into our heads by controlled conditions, while eating figs or dates, while drinking wine. "You must hear everything, or there will be a negative effect," our teacher said. But even though we had been warned, by the end of the lecture, there would always be the few who'd fallen fast asleep. And if they, the sleeping ones, were dreaming insanity's dream, in which memory is an arrow hanging frozen in the air, our hands and voices failed to reach them, even when we shook them and begged them and called them to come home.

TRUCE

The cinema, that rainy day, was warm and dry. Its film was silent. A horse was racing with a Model T among our stiff black coats and hats. The car puffed smoke. The white horse snorted. Then the film stopped. The crouching horseman had fallen half out of frame. Only in stillness like that, my friends, will God and Devil call their truce. Then it started up again, as if letting out a breath.

TONGUE

On Trnky Street I'd practice a certain word, walking to my classes at the Gimple school, and all the way back to my state-owned flat, saying it over and over—the tongue on the roof of my mouth like a transplant. You wanted to hear me say it, and when I got it exactly right eventually, it was like kissing you, you said, my tongue touching your tongue in the language.

TICK

The tick strides my bicep and hides in the shadowed hind leg of my tattoo of *The Tyger*. It lives off *The Tyger* tattoo for more than half my life, then it walks across my shoulders to the other arm, for the other half, and gorges on *The Lamb*. For the first half of my life, when I was drinking, I felt the lack; an ache; an emptiness I had to fill. For the second half, when I stopped drinking, I strove to be more emptiness than body. The problem then was surplus. How I would whine and bleat, to end my having. That too, quieted. The tick is moving toward the bare interior. It knows it has to die. There are no images or lights. We are coming to the end, when I will say a few words.

DISTANCE

The train passed over them and screeched to a stop. Later the tall man would tell the papers, "I saw someone in trouble" and "it was nothing." From under the train after a silence the two of them were whispering. "We're all right," the tall man said, raising his voice a little. It seemed to be called across a great distance. He still held the other man, whom he had saved, very tightly. Then the terminal went quiet and you could even hear the rats backing away on their little padded feet, as the train backed away, too.

TYPEWRITER

At the top of the old typewriter where the ribbon used to go, someone had threaded a spool of white bandage tape. No words had been typed over it though it was carefully aligned between the type guide and the black platen like a rolling pin, ready for a page to be inserted. I was told it had sat like this in the house for a hundred years since the end of the First World War, when typewriter ribbon was in shortage but bandages and medical supplies were made in surplus. I understand. The words do not describe anything. They only wrap themselves as evidence tightly around the invisible body, the invisible wound, the invisible genitals, the invisible hand.

THE WORLD TO COME

The warming has started. In the North, the dogs have grown so thin their bones show through. In the South, the parks lay flat as wet tablecloths. In the East, no more flying violinists. Instead there will be death announcements hammered onto the kiosks again, and the shoppers, their thin hair sprayed into saurian horns, dark henna red, will carry their bags to the meat shop as always, the bread shop as always, the Bull's Blood shop, as always, as always to the shop that sells the white cabbage. In the West, at the Automat, Edward Hopper's solitary customer has taken off a glove.

THE THIRD PERSON

One must speak of the eternal self in the third person only. The eternal self stood beneath the olive trees that wagged their branches. It lived off sunlight, once, and the gloppy impasto of rain. The eternal self once had hands and a face; eyes and a mouth. But snails ate up the grass. Then the sky; the sun. Until there was no world. No light. The body, invisible. All that remained were birds who knew how to fly at night, and snails and insects—instead of words that speak of an eternal self. Instead of the work of the hands.

ACKNOWLEDGMENTS

Thanks to the following journals in which the poems first appeared:

The American Journal of Poetry: "The Classical Age"
Bitter Oleander: "Astronomy"
The Cincinnati Review: "Danse Macabre"
Conduit: "Vocative Case," "Premise"
Copper Nickel: "During Snow," "Truce"
Dappled Things: "The Name of God"
december: "The World to Come"
Diode: "Tongue"
The Missouri Review: "The Sun," "The Moon," "Mercury," "Venus,"
   "Mars," "Jupiter," "Saturn"
Mudlark: "The Age of Radio," "Voyage," "Decay"
Palimpsest: "Fox," "Nostalgia"
Plume: "Before Snow," "The Age of the Onion"
RHINO: "Birthday"

"Three Tenement Rooms in Moravia" first appeared in my limited
edition selected and new poems, *The Long Answer.*

My gratitude to William Waltz and the editorial staff at Conduit Books
& Ephemera, as well as those who have led me by their example to
see more clearly, to listen with kind attention—my spiritual family
of living and late friends, colleagues, writers of supportive letters,
teachers, and students present and past. Finally, deep thanks to Judith
Bowles, Blas Falconer, Laura Reece Hogan, Ilya Kaminsky, Yusef
Komunyakaa, Katherine Larson, Laren McClung, Jenny Molberg, and
Carsten René Nielsen, who each read drafts of this collection in early
and late stages, and to the editors who helped me shape it along the
way. And to Sibylle Baier, whose generosity in the summer of 2020
when I needed a home in Lenox will remain in my heart.

ABOUT THE AUTHOR

David Keplinger is the author of several books of poetry, including most recently *Another City* (Milkweed Editions, 2018), which was awarded the 2019 UNT Rilke Prize for a mid-career poet. His other books of prose poetry include *The Prayers of Others* (New Issues Press, 2006), winner of the Colorado Book Award, and *The Most Natural Thing* (New Issues Press, 2013). In 2020 he was the recipient of the Emily Dickinson Award from the Poetry Society of America.

OTHER TITLES FROM CONDUIT BOOKS & EPHEMERA

Present Tense Complex by Suphil Lee Park
Sacrificial Metal by Esther Lee
The Miraculous, Sometimes by Meg Shevenock
The Last Note Becomes Its Listener by Jeffrey Morgan
Animul/Flame by Michelle Lewis